2002

Dear Tony,

You are your own
happy story.
Thanks for being such a
happy part of our journey.

Melanie &
Smp

12 True Stories For Happy Living

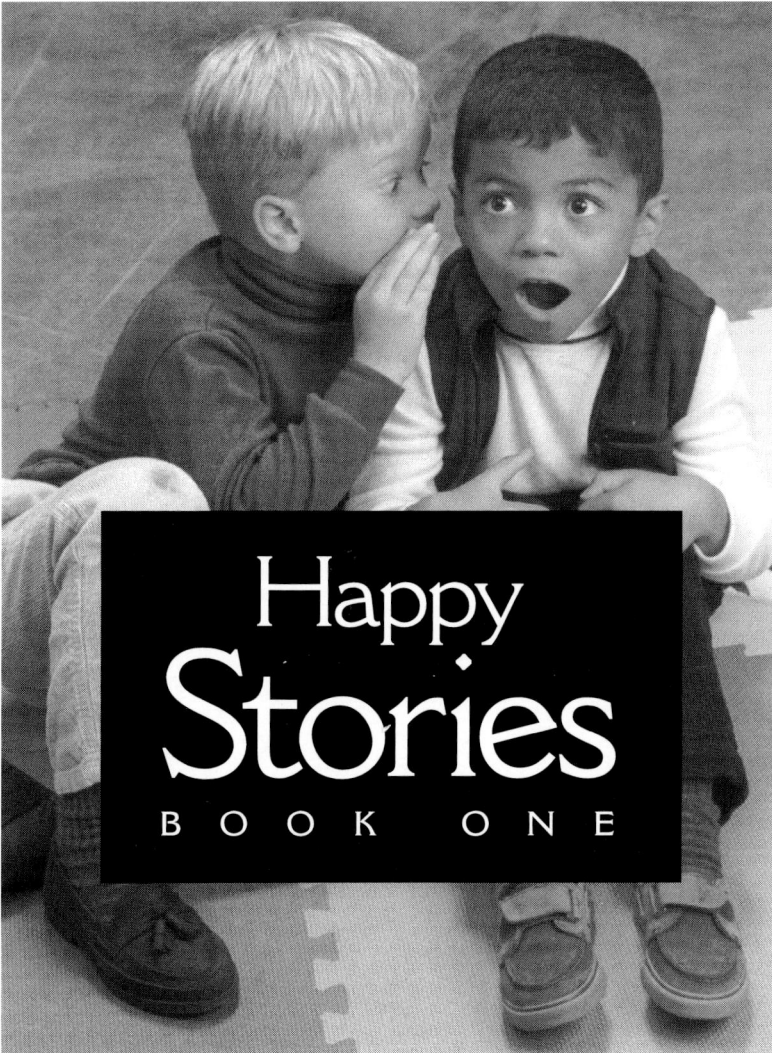

Happy Stories

BOOK ONE

Snip Francis and Melanie Gilbert

Photography by Ameen Howrani
Designed by Lisa Wissman and Heather Koskela
Edited by Brian J. Fisher
Published by Little Salamander Press

Published in the United States of America
Little Salamander Press
Penobscot Building
645 Griswold St.
P.O. Box 310759
Detroit, MI 48231
www.littlesalamanderpress.com

Francis, Snip/Gilbert, Melanie
Happy Stories: 12 True Stories for Happy Living
Photography by Ameen Howrani
Designed by Lisa Wissman and Heather Koskela
Edited by Brian J. Fisher

Summary:
These true, simple stories teach children how and why their actions
matter in the world. Through 12 adventures, the reader explores
themes of honesty, respect, perseverance, compassion and teamwork.
Even lessons can be happy stories.

ISBN: 1-890616-23-0
1. Humorous stories.   2. Parent and child – Juvenile literature.
3. Bedtime stories – Non-fiction.
Library of Congress Catalog Number 2002093833

Printed in the United States of America by Malloy
10 9 8 7 6 5 4 3 2 1

Little
Salamander
Press

To my Grossmutter,
who taught me
the art of storytelling and
the joy of happy living.

And to my Grandpa Gilbert,
who knew that good stories
live forever.

To my Sita and Gidu,
who gave life to generations
of happy stories.

Stories

A Revealing Story   1

Paying the Price   9

School Rules   17

Window Pain   25

The Right Step   33

Seeing the Light   41

All Fired Up   49

Weather or Not   57

Fishing for Success   65

The Big Picture   73

A Chilling Tale   81

In Too Deep   89

Acknowledgments

The St. Hilaire Family, Ron Kefgen, Don Gray and
Doug Luttenberger of Grosse Pointe Red Barons
for use of the football uniform, helmet and football
found opposite Page 1 and on page 5.

Cheryl Mackay Designs for use of the bracelet
found on Page 14.

Kathy Roberts of the Grosse Pointe Superintendent's
office for the use of the school desk found on Page 21.

Dr. Peter Francis and Louise DiMambro of Northpointe
Pediatrics for use of the surgical supplies found on Page 30.

The Gilbert, Francis, Ayrault and Monette families for
the use of the winter boots found on Page 36.

The John and Kim Francis family for use of their tent
and sleeping bags found on Page 44.

Curly, the horse of the Grosse Pointe Hunt Club Barn,
for the use of his hay found on Pages 48 and 52.

Ray Florkowski for use of his pitchfork found on Page 52.

Dr. John Ricci and Kim Isaacson for the use of the dental tray found on Page 76.

The Oleksik and Luther families for use of their toboggan found on Page 80.

The Lisa and Mike Monette family for use of their Flyer sled found on Page 80.

Stephanie for use of her floatie found on Page 94.

Mom and Dad Gilbert for the window found on Page 28, the vase and flowers found on Page 54, the door found on Page 84, the shovels found on Page 86, the rings found on Page 92, and for the donation of several large pizzas to feed 23 hungry kids during the day-long photo shoot.

The team at Xperience Communications for helping us make it happen.

Terry Ayrault of Watercooler Advertising for introducing us to Ameen Howrani.

Kelly Gregory Ross of Sidefx Productions, the videographer of "The Making of Happy Stories."

And, finally, to our 23 "models" for bringing *Happy Stories* to life.

Other books by
Snip Francis and Melanie Gilbert

Hey Look! The Happy Book

Authors' Notes

The Authors' Notes is our opportunity to do some story-telling about the people and the stories behind *Happy Stories*.

Snip and I both come from big families. Snip is the eighth of 10 children and I am the fourth of six. Her paternal grand-parents and my maternal grandparents immigrated to this country in the mid-1920s. They brought themselves and a boatload of stories to their new country.

Our stateside relatives, some of whom fought in the Revolutionary War, also had deep storytelling roots. It is into this rich heritage that we were born and nurtured.

We would like to thank our parents for providing such fertile ground from which we could grow our ideas into a book. In particular, I'd like to thank my mom and dad, Johanna and Ellwyn Gilbert, for always keeping the faith. Your love and support guided us.

That is a happy story all by itself.

We'd also like to thank our editor, Brian J. Fisher for his sharp eye and clear mind; our designers Lisa Wissman and Heather Koskela for making something out of nothing; and, finally, photographer Ameen Howrani, who shouldn't have but did.

Happy Stories is voices from the past speaking to the present and to the future. It's whispers of wisdom floating from one generation to the next.

Every family has stories to tell. These are ours.

Melanie Gilbert & Snip Francis

Happy
Stories

12 True Stories For Happy Living

BOOK ONE

A Revealing Story

P eter kicked the dirt and leaves gathered under the wooden bench where he was sitting. It was the fourth quarter and his team, the Red Barons, was playing for the league championship against the Blue Devils. It was the last game of the season and they were losing.

The Blue Devils' confidence had rattled the Red Barons and they had made lots of mistakes. Even Peter had made a couple of bad plays and Coach Ron had benched him at the half.

Peter shivered. Halloween was only a few days away, but it

already felt like winter. He peeked over his shoulder into the stands and looked for his family.

His Dad was sitting perfectly straight watching the game with his arms folded across his chest and his hands stuck underneath them for warmth.

His sister was sipping a cup of hot chocolate and his Mom was bundled in her favorite blanket. It was red and black — the team colors of the Red Barons. She saw Peter, waved enthusiastically and then blew him a kiss.

"Aw, Mom," Peter muttered. He gave her a quick little wave and then glanced down the bench to see if any of his teammates had noticed. But they were intently watching the action on the field as the Blue Devils' quarterback fired the football up the middle to a waiting receiver.

"They're going to score again," groaned Peter and he angrily unsnapped his chin strap from his helmet. But suddenly, the crowd behind him leapt to their feet cheering and his teammates were jumping up and down on the sidelines. His friend Adam ran up to him and pounded Peter's shoulder pads with his fists excitedly.

"He dropped the ball! He dropped the ball!" yelled Adam, and butted his helmet against Peter's helmet. The two friends ran to the sideline to watch the next play.

The Blue Devils had time for only one more play and they lined up to kick a field goal. The ball sailed through the uprights for three points. The score was Blue Devils 17, Red Barons 13, with only three minutes left in the game.

Coach Ron called his players together.

"Team," Coach said, "this is a tough opponent, but they just gave us a big chance to win this game. I know you can do it, so go out there and show them that you're winners. Hands in, and on the count of three … One. Two. Three … ."

"GO BARONS!" the team shouted, throwing their hands in the air.

"Peter," called Coach Ron. "I'm putting you back in the game, but you need to focus. You have to keep your eyes on the ball. You got that?"

"I got it, Coach," Peter said.

The Red Barons were fired up and the other team sensed it. In three plays, the Red Barons moved the ball up the field to the 50-yard line.

On the next play, Adam made a tremendous block that allowed a Red Barons running back to gain another 25 yards. They could see the goal line.

But the Blue Devils regrouped and drove the Red Barons back 10 yards on one play and five yards on the next. Peter looked at the scoreboard. Only one minute left to play and he still hadn't gotten the ball.

Then the Red Barons' quarterback faked a pass and instead ran the ball for 20 yards.

Now they were in their "Red Zone." Coach Ron called a time-out.

"We're out of time, team. We've got to score on the next play. Peter, the ball's coming to you."

Peter glanced back at the field. The goal post seemed a long way away. There were only 22 seconds on the clock and the other team looked bigger and meaner than before. Then he remembered what Coach had said about staying focused on each play. Peter swallowed hard.

"I can do it, Coach," he said determinedly.

Adam ran up to Peter as they lined up on the field.

"Peter, I've got your back," he said grinning, as he took his position.

The fans in the stands were on their feet and the noise was deafening. Even his Dad was shouting and his Mom and sister held up a sign that said, "#45 IS A STAR."

Peter's face flushed and he felt warm all over. His heart was pounding and he wiped his sweaty hands vigorously on his pants. The opposing player scowled at him. He blinked hard a couple of times and pushed his mouth guard into place.

Focus, focus, focus, he repeated to himself. He heard the snap and he took off running down the field.

Adam blocked one opposing player, then another. "Run, Peter, run!" he yelled.

Peter could see the goal line. He looked over his shoulder and saw the quarterback throw the ball. It arced high in the air then started floating down toward him. Peter stretched out his hands when he heard a loud pop and felt his belt buckle bounce off his knee. He felt his pants loosen with each step and they slipped a little off his waist. Peter could feel the cold air on his skin. As the ball dropped closer and closer, his pants dropped lower and lower.

Peter's mind was racing. If he caught the ball, he'd drop his pants. But if he caught his pants, he'd drop the ball. His pants fell some more.

He gritted his teeth. "Focus," he said out loud. The ball was inches from his hands.

Peter reached up, grabbed the football and dove across the goal line. The Red Barons' fans went crazy. Adam raced over to his friend.

"You did it, Peter. We won. We won the game," screamed Adam.

Adam helped Peter to his feet. Peter held the game-winning football in one hand and his pants up in the other.

"Well, buddy, I gotta tell you — that was some play," marveled Adam.

The rest of the team charged down the field and mobbed

Peter. When they finished celebrating, the Red Barons lined up to shake hands with the Blue Devils.

In the locker room after the game, Coach Ron made his customary speech.

"You can be proud of the way you played today," he said. "But, Peter, your extra effort won this game. That's why I'm naming you the game's Most Valuable Player. Congratulations!"

Peter shook Coach Ron's hand.

"Coach," said Peter, "I kept my focus like you said. But thanks to your advice, I almost lost my pants out there, too."

And the whole locker room erupted into cheers and laughter.

Most Valuable Player

The Red Barons

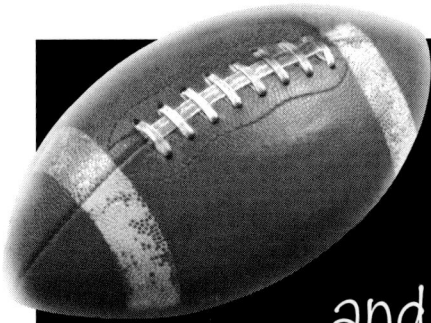

Keep your eye
on the ball
and finish what
you started.

Hey Look!
HUCKLEBERRY FINN
Mark Twain
STUART LITTLE
The Busy, Busy World of Richard Scarry
THE SECRET OF THE OLD CLOCK

Paying the Price

"Five dollars!" exclaimed Jacqueline. "Aunt Kay gave you five dollars?"

Hannah grinned and waved the money over her head.

"But, why?" Jac asked her cousin.

"I earned it," said Hannah.

"How?"

"Remember when it was really hot last week?"

Jac nodded. It had been so hot, the citronella candles had melted and left a big, gooey mess all over their back porch.

"Aunt Kay said if I watered her flowers every day after school, she'd pay me five dollars."

"That's a dollar a day," calculated Jac. "Are you going to buy something with it?"

"I'm going to buy a book. Do you want to go with me?"

The cousins rode to the bookstore. As Jac locked the bikes to the rack, her bracelet fell off.

"Not again!" she exclaimed. "Hannah, can you help me with this?"

Hannah slid the little ring through the loop on the other end and closed the clasp. Then they went inside and settled down in front of the intermediate books where *Nancy Drew*, *The Adventures of Huckleberry Finn* and the *Little House* series were shelved.

Hannah loved books. And now that it was almost summer break, she'd have lots of time to read.

"Here's a book of funny poems," said Jac.

They took turns reading the silly rhymes. They were laughing so hard, they didn't hear their neighbors, Cameron and Riley, come up.

"What's so funny?" asked Cameron, balancing a stack of books and movies in his arms.

"Cameron, are you buying all that stuff?" asked Hannah, ignoring his question.

"Kind of. Me and Riley are using our gift cards to buy it." The brothers grinned at each other, delighted with their shared fortune.

"How much do you have?" asked Jac.

"Fifty dollars," shouted Riley.

Cameron laughed. "Hey, you guys can come over later and watch movies if you want," he offered.

Jac and Hannah watched as the boys headed off to the register.

"Fifty dollars," said Jac. "That's a lot of money."

"Yeah, I know," replied Hannah, pulling her crumpled five-dollar bill out of her pocket.

"Well, how much do books cost?" wondered Jac.

They studied the stickers on the back of the books. The mystery book cost sixteen dollars, the book of poems cost seventeen dollars and the book about wizards cost almost eighteen dollars.

"I don't think I can buy *any* books," said a disappointed Hannah.

"Wait a minute, Hannah — what about these books over here?" Jac walked to the paperback section a row away. "See, this one's only $4.95."

Hannah read the back cover. It said this was a story about pioneer life in the Wild West with characters like Annie Oakley, Buffalo Bill and the famous Sioux chief Sitting Bull.

"This looks pretty good," she said with surprise.

They got in line just as Cameron and Riley finished checking out. The brothers had so much stuff that the book clerk had to put it in two big bags.

"Next in line," called Ms. Hile.

Hannah and Jac eyed the magnets, sticker packs, candy, finger puppets and bookmarks on the counter as Ms. Hile rang up their purchase. Everything was so expensive! Hannah slid her five dollars on top of her book.

"Your total is $5.25," said Ms. Hile.

"But it says $4.95," protested Hannah.

Ms. Hile smiled. "Yes," she said. "But I have to charge you sales tax, too."

Hannah couldn't believe it. She couldn't even buy this book, either!

"Hannah, you can borrow my quarter," said Jac, reaching deep into her pocket and handing the coin to Ms. Hile.

"Excuse me," said Ms. Hile and she stepped away to answer the phone. When she came back, she put the quarter in the register and placed Hannah's book in a bag. The girls left the store and sat down by their bikes.

"Thanks, Jac," said Hannah. She pulled her book out of the bag and the five-dollar bill fell out onto the ground.

"Hannah," said Jac, "I think she forgot to take your money."

Hannah picked up the crumpled cash. "Do you think she put it in there on purpose?"

Jac just shrugged.

"If we take it back, she might get in trouble for making such a big mistake," suggested Hannah.

Jac nodded thoughtfully.

"She should have been more careful, though, don't you think?" asked Hannah.

"Is this like Finders Keepers?" asked Jac.

They sat there quietly studying the five-dollar bill.

"We could get some ice cream with your money," suggested Jac.

"I could buy my mom some candy," said Hannah. "That would be nice, right?"

"Sure," said Jac.

The girls were quiet again.

"Maybe I should go back in and give her the money," said Hannah finally.

"Yeah, maybe you should," sighed Jac.

The girls went back to the counter and waited patiently while Ms. Hile finished helping another customer.

"Hello, girls," she said. "Did you forget something?"

The words came rushing out as Hannah pushed her money hurriedly across the counter.

"Well, I found this five dollars in my bag and I thought maybe you forgot to take it when I bought my book and so I'm bringing it back."

Ms. Hile was surprised. "I did? My goodness, sometimes it gets so busy in here … thank you so much." She put the money in the register.

"I think I have something that belongs to one of you, too," said Ms. Hile.

"You do?" asked Hannah.

Ms. Hile took something out of a drawer and laid it on the counter.

"Jac! Your bracelet," shouted Hannah.

Jac looked at the bracelet on the counter and then at the empty spot around her wrist.

"A customer found it on the floor just after you girls left so I put it in the Lost and Found," said Ms. Hile. "I was hoping you would come back for it."

"Thank you," said Jac, stuffing the troublesome bracelet in her pocket.

"You're welcome," said Ms. Hile.

The girls got on their bikes and pedaled for home.

"She didn't even know that you didn't pay," said Jac.

"I know," said Hannah proudly, "but now she knows that we did."

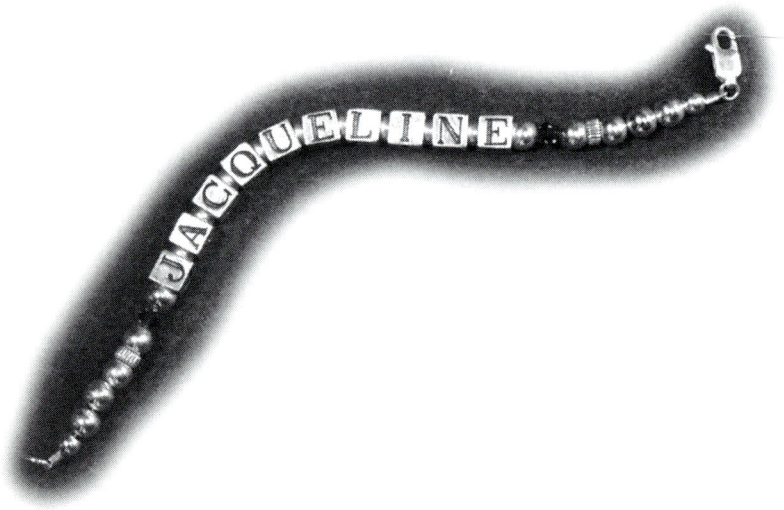

You can't
buy character:
Treat people like
you want to be treated.

School Rules

"Hey, Abbie," whispered David to his classmate, "do you want to be on my basketball team in gym?"

"David, please. No talking," said his teacher, Ms. Kamin.

The students were working quietly on their spelling words until recess. But he was already finished. What's taking everyone so long, he wondered?

David leaned to his right, "Hody, do you want to eat lunch together?"

Ms. Kamin came up the aisle. "David, please do not

bother Hody."

David watched the clock. Tick, tock, tick, tock. It was moving so slowly.

He tapped the shoulder of the boy in front of him.

"Kurt, bring in your trading cards tomorrow, OK?"

Ms. Kamin tapped David on the shoulder. He looked up tentatively. "David, I don't want to tell you again. Please stop talking."

He sat still for a while, looking out the window and thinking about recess. Maybe he would swing on the monkey bars. Naw, too cold. Maybe he would play field hockey. No, can't do that, either, he thought. I forgot my stick. Hmm, maybe I can borrow Cricket's stick.

David turned around to the girl behind him.

"Cricket, can I borrow your hockey stick?" David asked.

"David!" thundered Ms. Kamin. "Put your head down on your desk right now."

The whole class stopped what they were doing and looked at David. His face turned beet red.

"Now!" said Ms. Kamin.

"Oh, all right," groused David. He folded his arms across the top of the desk and put his head down.

BRRRING! It was the recess bell. At last! David started to get out of his chair when he felt his teacher's hand on his shoulder.

"I'm sorry, David, but I'm afraid you have detention instead of recess," she said.

His classmates grabbed their winter coats and ran outside. David sat at his desk while Ms. Kamin graded papers.

"You are a very good speller, David," she said. "Every one of

your spelling words is correct."

There was a knock on the door and Principal Jaros came in with a student David didn't recognize.

"Hello, David," she said.

"Hi, Principal Jaros," said David politely.

"Ms. Kamin," said the principal, "This is Isaac. He is a new student to Oak Elementary. I wonder if you have someone in your class who will make Isaac feel welcome and explain the school rules to him."

Ms. Kamin smiled. "I have the perfect person," she said.

"Thank you," said Principal Jaros and she returned to her office.

Ms. Kamin introduced David to Isaac.

"David," said Ms. Kamin. "I would like you to be Isaac's guide."

"What do I do?" asked David.

"You'll be his friend and helper for the rest of the day," she explained.

Their classmates returned from recess and the students began their geography lesson.

"Where did you used to live?" David asked Isaac.

"In Michigan," answered Isaac. He pointed to it on the map. "See how it looks like a big mitten? That's because it's surrounded by the Great Lakes."

"Chicago is on Lake Michigan," noted David. "And that's a Great Lake. But that's the only one I can remember."

"I know a good trick to remember all five lakes," said Isaac.

"What is it?" asked David.

"Just remember the word 'HOMES.' That stands for

Huron, Ontario, Michigan, Erie and Superior."

David repeated the names of the lakes. "That is a good trick," he said. "Where did you live in Michigan?"

"In Detroit," answered Isaac.

David traced his finger from Detroit all the way to Chicago.

"Wow. You moved a long way," he said.

It was time for lunch and David was surprised that the morning had gone by so quickly. He and Isaac sat in the cafeteria and ate their lunches.

"Where do you live now?" asked David, taking a drink of his chocolate milk.

"On South Washington Street," Isaac replied.

"That's right by my house!" exclaimed David. "Maybe we can walk home together."

The bell rang and lunch was over.

"David, aren't you going to eat your apple?" wondered Isaac.

"Nope. I'm going to give it to someone," he said.

"Who?" asked Isaac.

"I have the perfect person," smiled David.

They returned to their classroom for afternoon storytime. David stopped by Ms. Kamin's desk and handed her his apple.

"Why, thank you, David," said Ms. Kamin. She set the apple on her desk. "I'll have this for my afternoon snack. It seems you are doing a good job of explaining things to Isaac," she said.

David joined Isaac on the storytime mat. They listened as Ms. Kamin read *Stuart Little*."

"David, isn't Stuart funny," said Isaac.

David nodded, but didn't answer. He was trying to listen to

the story.

"David," whispered Isaac. "I have a cat. Her name is Meowser."

David shifted position and leaned forward a little bit so he could hear Ms. Kamin better.

"Hey," said Isaac again, tapping David's leg, "do you like soccer?"

David leaned in close to Isaac. He put his hand in front of his mouth so nobody would hear him.

"Isaac," he whispered directly into his ear, "we're not supposed to talk during storytime. Let's wait until recess."

"Oh," said a surprised Isaac.

During recess, the boys kicked the soccer ball back and forth.

"Hey, Isaac," asked David, "why *is* your cat called Meowser?"

Just then the bell rang and recess was over.

"I guess I'll have to tell you on our walk home, huh?" smiled Isaac.

"I guess so," laughed David.

Here's a rule
to live by: There's
a time and place
for everything.

Window Pain

It was a school night and the Borrego girls were doing their homework while their little sister, Natalia, colored pictures.

"Spell 'hundred'," said Carly, drilling her sister, Carmen, in her spelling words.

Carmen spelled it correctly.

"OK, now spell 'knew.' "

Carmen said, "New, n-e-w, new."

Carly started laughing.

"What's so funny?" demanded Carmen who was proud of

how well she could spell.

"Homophones are words that sound the same but mean different things," explained Carly. "I'll give it to you in a sentence: 'Carmen knew how to spell new.' "

"Oh, I get it," smiled Carmen. "Knew, k-n-e-w, knew. What about *blew* a bubble and a *blue* crayon?" she asked, taking one from Natalia.

"Hey!" fussed Natalia, yanking back her crayon.

"That's one," laughed Carly. "And so is '*hey*, cut it out,' and the *hay* that horses eat." She gave her little sister a pat on the back. "Good one, Natalia."

Natalia giggled at being included in the funny word game.

Mrs. Borrego came into the living room. "How's the homework coming, girls?" she asked.

"I finished my spelling words, Mom," bragged Carmen.

"I only have one more math problem and I'm done, too," reported Carly.

"And what about you, Natalia? Did you finish coloring your picture?"

Natalia waved her drawing at her Mom.

"It's beautiful," smiled Mrs. Borrego. "Girls, I need to cover the plants in the backyard to protect them from the frost tonight. Please get ready for bed. I'll be back in a little bit to tuck you in." They heard the back door shut.

Carly finished her math and Carmen helped Natalia put away her crayons. Then they all went upstairs and put on their pajamas.

"Carly," gurgled Carmen, her mouth full of toothpaste, "please hang my *clothes* in the closet and *close* the door."

"I *threw* them on the floor because I'm *through* helping you," retorted Carly, continuing the word play.

Carmen came into the bedroom, "I *hear* voices but nobody's *here*." She deliberately bumped into Carly who was sitting on the floor brushing Natalia's hair into pigtails.

"Oh, yeah!" answered Carly. She grabbed her pillow and playfully whacked Carmen on the legs.

Carmen snatched her pillow off her bed. "*Wait* 'til you feel the *weight* of this." Thump! Her pillow landed on Carly's back.

Carly jumped up and lifted her pillow over her head taking aim at Carmen.

"You guys better stop it," warned Natalia. "Mom's gonna be mad."

But her older sisters were having too much fun to listen. Carly's pillow hit Carmen's shoulder with a thud. Feathers slipped out and floated around the room. Natalia tried to make them stop but was knocked to the floor. She watched as the pillows flew back and forth over her head.

"Guys, stop it," she pleaded again.

Crash! Carmen's pillow missed Carly and hit the dresser instead. Brushes and knickknacks went flying.

"Oh, no," moaned Natalia. She crawled out of the way and up onto the safety of a bed.

Carmen trapped Carly by the bedroom window. But Carly wound up and swung first.

"Hiya!" yelled Carmen. She kicked out her leg to deflect her sister's fast-approaching pillow. The kick knocked the pillow out of Carly's hands. Carly ducked as her sister's leg came hurtling toward her. Carmen tried to stop but instead

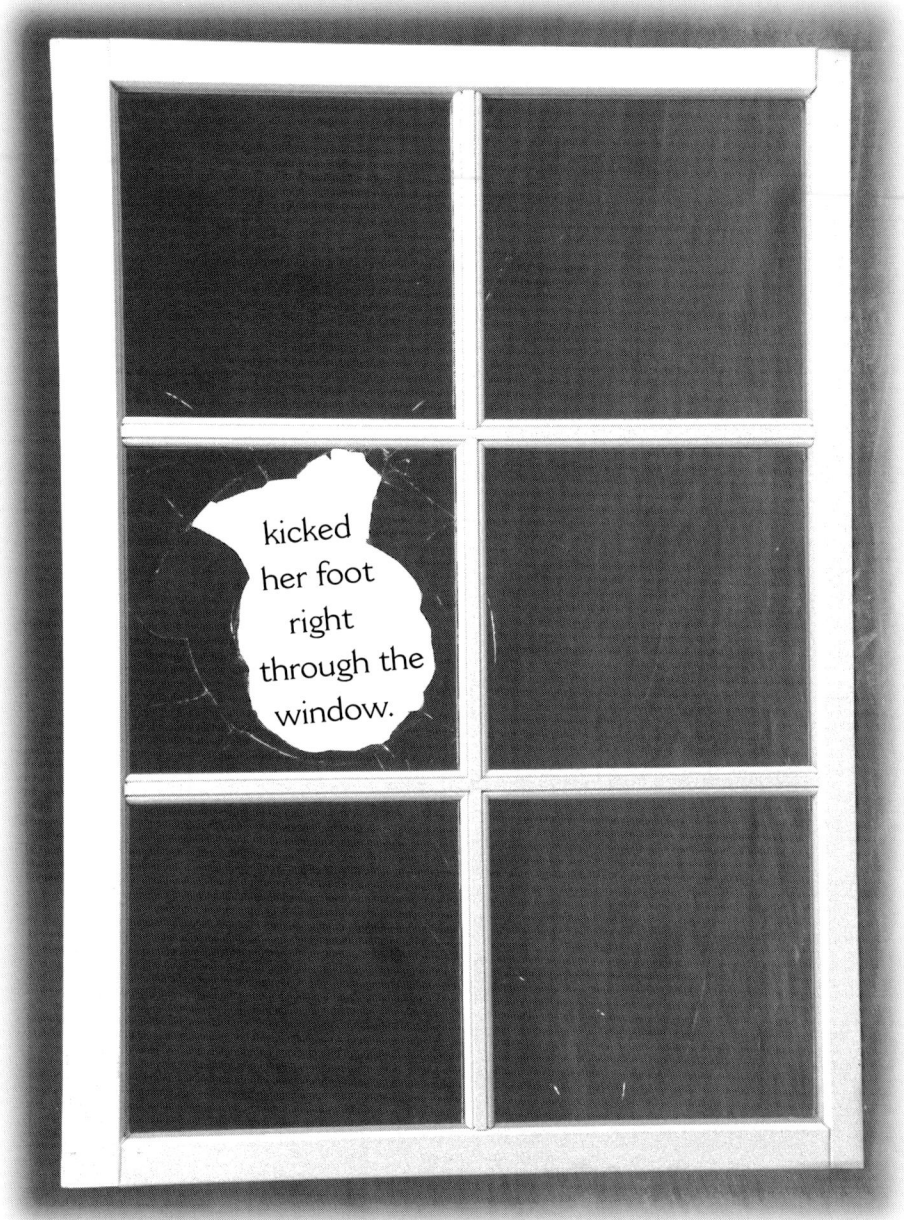

kicked
her foot
right
through the
window.

Mrs. Borrego heard the glass shatter and ran into the house. Carmen was sitting on the floor holding her bleeding foot.

"Carly, you and Natalia run next door to Dr. Brian's house," she ordered. Mrs. Borrego wrapped a pillowcase around Carmen's foot and tied a loose knot on top. Then she scooped up her daughter, started down the stairs and headed out the door.

Dr. Brian was waiting for them on his front porch. They followed him into his kitchen.

"Mrs. Borrego, sit down with her in your lap and prop up her foot on the table."

Natalia and Carly watched from the doorway as Dr. Brian took a silver tray out of the cupboard and lined it with a sterile cloth. He opened his black bag and pulled out a little bottle of clear liquid, a pair of tweezers, some gauze, a bottle of iodine, two scissors, a package of black thread and a syringe with a long needle. Natalia covered her eyes.

"Now, you're going to feel a little pinch and then you won't feel anything else," said Dr. Brian. He snapped on a pair of surgical gloves and filled the needle with the clear liquid. He tapped the syringe and squirted a little out. "Ready?"

Carmen nodded slowly, her eyes brimming with tears.

"The good news is that I don't see any glass in there," Dr. Brian said. "But I'm going to have to give you about five stitches."

"All done," he said after awhile, pulling off his gloves.

Mrs. Borrego thanked Dr. Brian and they headed home. She taped a piece of cardboard over the foot-sized hole in the window and put a pillow under Carmen's foot to keep it elevated through the night.

"We'll talk about this in the morning," she said as she tucked them into bed and shut off the light.

"Carmen," whispered Carly. "That was quite a *feat* with your *feet*."

"Yeah, well, if you weren't such a *pain*, I wouldn't have kicked that *pane* of glass," chuckled Carmen.

They were quiet for a moment.

"Maybe next time, we'll just stick to word games," said Carly.

"Good idea," yawned Carmen.

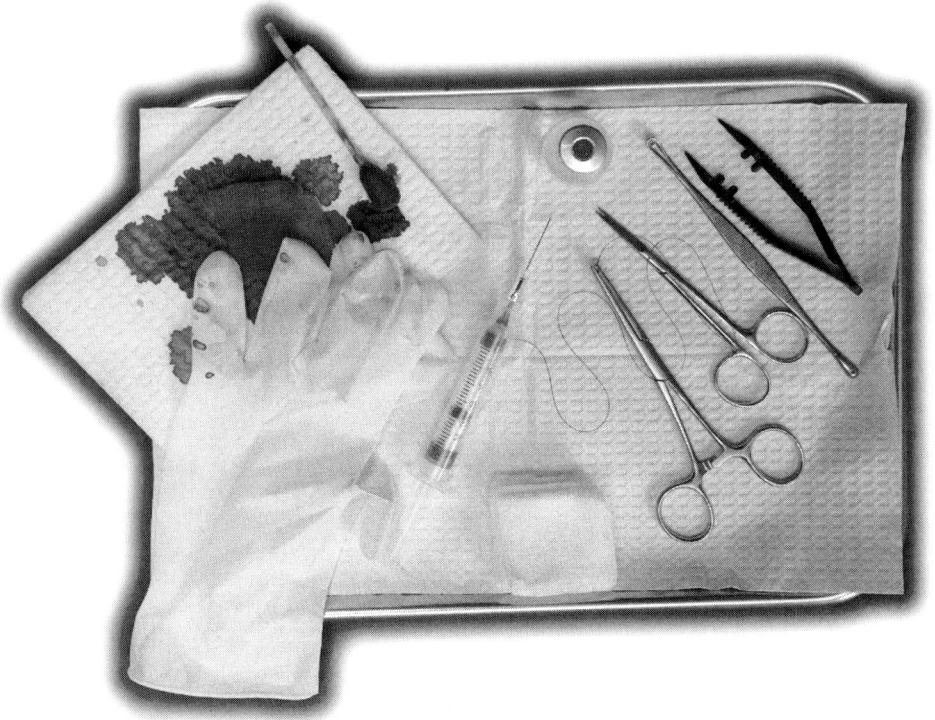

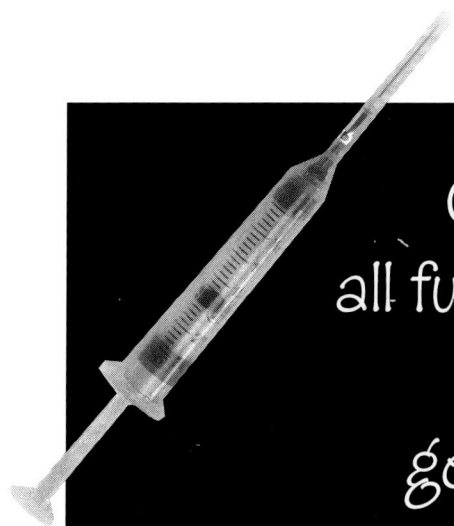

Ouch! It's
all fun and games
until someone
gets hurt.

The Right Step

Joey laid out 22 slices of frozen bread. He spread peanut butter over half the pieces and plopped two tablespoons of jelly on the rest. Then he matched a peanut butter piece against a jelly piece, cut it in two, wrapped it in wax paper, and placed it inside one of the ten brown paper bags lined up on the kitchen counter.

Each bag got one sandwich — except for Nicole's bag. His older sister got two sandwiches because she had swim practice every day after school.

Joey wrote his name on one bag and set it by his backpack. Then he wrote Nicole, Dan, Debbie, Gerard, Lisa, George, Ellen, Kristen and Maureen in black magic marker on the others.

Finally! He thought. He sat down and poured himself a big bowl of cereal with milk.

"What a beautiful morning," said Mrs. Mac Donald. Joey's mom opened a kitchen window and let the sweet, warm air flow into the room. "You'd never know it was the middle of winter."

One by one, his siblings grabbed their lunch bags off the counter and headed to school.

"Come on, Joey, or we'll be late," said Nicole.

"Kids, wear your boots," said Mrs. Mac Donald, "a big winter storm is headed this way."

"Mom, it's like springtime out there," complained Nicole.

"I know. But this is the calm before the storm and it could change in a hurry."

Their boots were too bulky to carry so Nicole and Joey put them on and stuffed their shoes inside their backpacks.

"My feet are *boiling*," whined Joey, as they stomped down the street.

"You can put your shoes on when you get to school, Joey," said Nicole.

"Nice boots, Joey," yelled his friend, Terry. He ran up and kicked Joey's boot with his sneaker.

"Cut it out, Terry. My mom made me," groused Joey.

He did feel silly wearing his big winter boots when it was so warm outside. He unzipped his coat and stuffed his gloves in his pocket. Once he got to school, he put on his shoes and

34

threw his boots inside his locker.

The day became warmer and warmer. That afternoon, the gym teacher brought out the basketballs, soccer balls and kick- balls and held class outside.

"If you make the last out you have to wear Joey's boots home," taunted Terry during the kickball game. All the kids laughed and Joey smiled weakly, trying hard to be a good sport.

By the time school let out, the sun was still shining in the clear, blue sky. The kids flooded the hallways with excited energy. Joey stared at his winter boots filling the bottom of his locker. He was putting them on when his friend Terry walked up.

"Hey, Joey," said Terry, "are you going to bring your sled to school tomorrow, too?" He playfully punched Joey in the arm.

"Very funny, Terry," snapped Joey. He was tired of being a good sport. Why did his mom make him wear these ridiculous boots anyway?

The hallways cleared out before Joey remembered that Nicole had swim practice and wouldn't be walking home with him. I'm not wearing these home, he thought. He took off his boots and crammed them back into his locker. He ran home wearing his shoes, feeling light and comfortable.

Joey was working on an English essay in the kitchen when Nicole came home from swim practice. She took off her boots and set them in the line by the back door.

"There are only nine pairs of boots, here, Joey. Who isn't home, yet?"

Joey hunched over his paper and pretended not to hear her.

"Joey," said Nicole, "I think your boots are missing. Did you forget them at school?"

Joey put down his pencil and held his finger to his lips.

"Shhh. Don't let Mom hear you," he whispered. "I left them at school on purpose, Nicole. It's not going to snow. Besides, I felt stupid wearing my boots and everybody was making fun of me."

"I hope you're right," said Nicole and she went upstairs to do her homework.

Joey's mom shook him awake the next morning.

"Wake up, sleepyhead."

Joey stretched and yawned as his mom opened the window blinds.

"Look at that snow," she said peering out the window. "And to think it was so nice yesterday."

He worried all through breakfast. How was he going to walk to school without his boots?

"Kids," called Mrs. Mac Donald, as Joey and Nicole got ready to leave for school, "don't forget to wear your boots." She laughed. "But I guess I don't have to tell you that today, do I?"

"Joey," whispered Nicole, "don't worry. Just follow behind me, OK?"

It's so cold, thought Joey, and he shivered as he stepped out onto the frozen, snow-covered ground.

Nicole stomped her foot into the snow and rocked it back and forth, making a little crater. "You just step into that and follow me, Joey. I'll be your boots," she said.

They walked the whole way to school like that — Nicole carefully making one big footprint after another and Joey following along behind her. They got to school just as the bell rang.

Joey saw Terry in class. "I guess I should have brought my sled to school today, huh?" he said good-naturedly to his friend.

"Yeah, and I should have worn my boots," grumbled Terry.

Joey looked under the desk at Terry's soggy sneakers. Little chunks of ice were melting from his laces.

After classes that day, Joey opened his locker and smiled as he pulled on his warm, dry boots.

"Terry, wait up!" yelled Joey as his friend passed him in the hallway. "Why don't we walk home together. You can follow in my footsteps."

Later, when Joey got home, he stomped his boots outside the door before lining them up in his spot against the wall.

"I've been keeping this warm for you," said his mom.

She put a mug of hot chocolate with whipped cream on the kitchen table.

"Where have you been?" she asked.

Joey wrapped his hands around the warm mug and took a sip.

"Oh, just helping a friend," he said.

You leave
    a big footprint
when you take
    care of others.

Seeing the Light

"Come on, kids — hurry up! We have work to do." Mr. Bergman waited, but no one responded.

"Steve! Eric! Michael! Heather! Maria!" he shouted. "Get back here this instant."

Slowly, they emerged from the woods.

"But, Dad, we were playing hide-and-go-seek," Heather said.

"I thought camping was supposed to be fun," complained Michael.

"Now, now," chided Mr. Bergman. "I need help with the laundry and the hammock, and your Mom needs help collecting kindling for the fire and some big sticks, too."

"Why?" asked Maria, the youngest.

"So we can roast marshmallows after dinner," said Mrs. Bergman.

"Marshmallows!" exclaimed the kids.

In no time, clothes were drying on the line, the hammock was swinging between two big oak trees, and macaroni and cheese was cooking on the fire.

After dinner, seven sticks roasted marshmallows over flickering embers.

"This camping stuff isn't so bad, is it kids?" asked Mrs. Bergman.

Michael carried a lantern and Heather held her flashlight so they could see their way back from the wash house on the moonless night. It was too hot in the tent, so they moved their sleeping bags outside. Michael was an amateur astronomer, and he pointed out constellations to his younger sister.

"That one over there, that's called the Ursa Major or the Big Dipper. See how it looks like a big cup with a long handle?"

"What's that really bright one above it?" asked Heather.

"Oh, that's the North Star or Polaris. It's the tip of Ursa Minor also called the Little Dipper." Michael looked at his sister. "See it?" he asked. She did see it and then she saw something else — a bright flash that overwhelmed the shining stars.

"Michael! I just saw lightning. I think it's going to rain. Maybe we should go inside."

"What! No way, Heather. It's perfectly clear. Besides, I don't

hear any thunder." He yawned. "I'm sleepy. Goodnight." He rolled over and fell asleep.

Flash! There it was again. She was sure it was lightning. She wiggled out of her sleeping bag.

"Dad, wake up," she whispered.

"Huh?" he said groggily.

"Dad, I just saw lightning. I think it's going to rain. Maybe we should roll up the car windows."

Mr. Bergman poked his head out of the tent and saw a sky full of twinkling stars.

"It's probably heat lightning," he explained, rubbing his eyes. "Sometimes you'll see it on a hot night with a clear sky. It's nothing. Go back to sleep."

Heather snuggled back in her sleeping bag. Flash! She sat up. This time it was so bright she could see her swimsuit on the clothesline. She crept back into the tent.

"Mom, are you awake?"

"What is it, honey?"

"Mom, I just saw lightning. I think it's going to rain. Maybe we should get the clothes and the hammock."

"Oh, sweetie, I think you were dreaming. Why don't I tuck you back into bed."

"No, Mom. I saw it. I did." They tiptoed out of the tent. Heather struggled to stay awake to show her Mom the lightning, but her eyes got too heavy and she fell fast asleep.

Heather woke suddenly. She heard something — a low rumbling sound. She peered at the sky. Where did that North Star go? Suddenly, a bolt of lightning illuminated the entire campground.

"Michael! Get up!" She shook her brother's shoulder. "We have to get in the tent now!"

Heather and Michael scrambled out of their sleeping bags and into the tent. The commotion woke everyone and Eric grumbled as they stepped on him.

Heather counted, "One one-thousand, two one-thousand, three one-thousand ... ."

She counted all the way up to twenty one-thousands when — KABOOM!!! Thunder shook the ground. Moments later, there was a flash of light so bright they could see each other's anxious faces. Heather started counting again.

"Heather, why are you counting?" Maria asked.

Heather counted up to fifteen when a huge clap of thunder boomed. Maria covered her ears.

"You count the number of seconds between the lightning and the thunder. When you divide that number by five, it tells you how many miles you are from the storm," explained Heather.

Plop. Seven heads looked up at the roof of the tent at the same time. Plop. Plop. Steve stuck his arm out the front flap and pulled in Michael and Heather's sleeping bags. Plop. Plop. Plop.

"Here it comes," he said wiping his wet hand on a bandanna and zipping shut the tent. Lightning flashed not once, but three times in a row. Heather hadn't even counted to five when the thunder exploded overhead. The kids shrieked and Maria jumped into her Mom's lap. Rain pounded the tent and the wind blew so fiercely it sounded like it was howling. They heard trees groaning and branches breaking. It seemed as if the storm was right over their heads.

"I told you it was going to rain," Heather shouted above the noise.

But nobody said a word and they all huddled in the middle of the tent away from the muddy water that started seeping in around the sides.

After awhile, the time between the lightning and the thunder got longer and longer and only a pitter-patter of raindrops softly slapped the tent.

"I think it's over," said Heather, who was quietly counting the time between each flash and boom.

"I think you're right," said her Dad. "There's nothing we can do tonight, so let's all try to get some sleep." When Heather crawled out of the tent that morning, the hammock had been ripped in half by a fallen tree branch and the clothes were

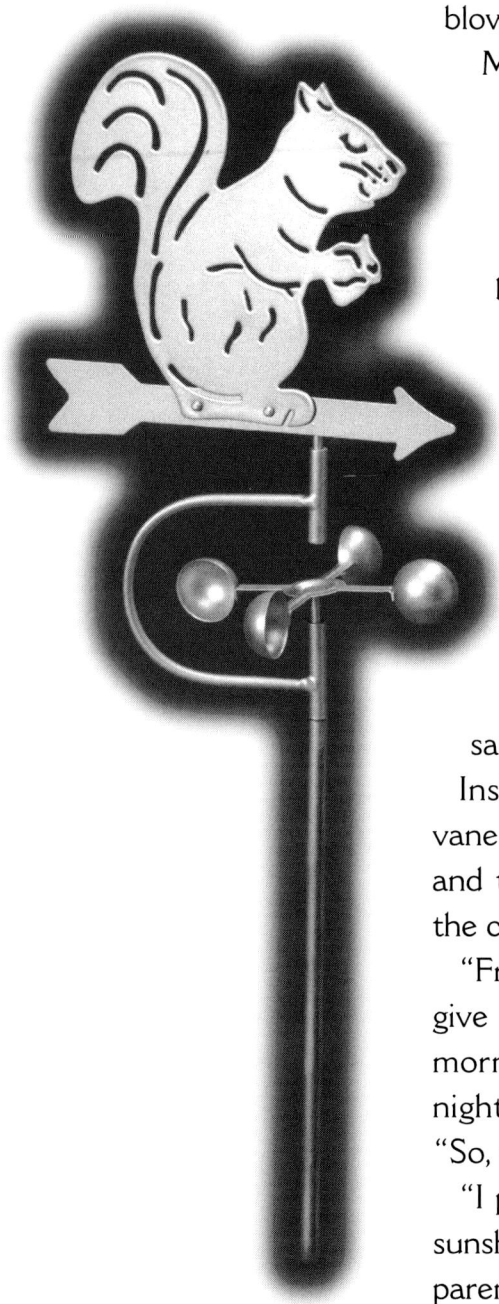

blown off the clothesline. Her Mom fished a swimsuit out of a puddle and plucked a towel off the top of the tent. Heather found Michael's cup and toothbrush buried in mud. Michael and her Dad returned from a trip to town and Heather giggled at the wet spots on the seat of their pants when they got out of the car.

"Heather, we have something for you." Her Dad held out a paper sack. "Open it."

Inside was a shiny weather vane. Heather stuck it in the mud and the little cups spun slowly in the cool breeze.

"From now on, you're going to give us a weather report every morning and especially every night," declared Mr. Bergman. "So, what's today's forecast?"

"I predict clear skies and lots of sunshine," she said, smiling at her parents and brother.

When you
believe in yourself,
others will
see the light.

All Fired Up

"It sure is hot," sighed Chelsea. She took off her straw hat and wiped her arm across her sweaty forehead. "I wish it would rain."

"Me, too," said her younger sister, Allie. "But Pop says, 'Wet hay bends, dry hay breaks.'"

"I know," replied Chelsea. She squinted up at the blazing July sun. They could forget about any shade, either — there wasn't a cloud in the sky.

"What's good for the hay, isn't so good for me," Chelsea said finally. She swept her blonde hair off her face and retied her two ponytails.

The girls knew that no farmer wanted rain during haying season. Wet hay couldn't be baled or stored in the barn. And without hay, there wouldn't be any bedding or food for the animals.

"Maybe we should try thinking about Curly and Toby, instead," suggested Allie. "They love it when we muck out their stalls and lay down fresh hay."

The girls were in charge of bringing in the hay from their field to feed and bed their horses. They had cut the hay and raked it out to dry. Now they were pitching it into 6-foot stacks.

They stopped for a minute and looked for their horses. Curly was nibbling at some of the grass poking through the fencing. Chelsea's horse, Toby, stood in the shade of a tree flicking flies with his tail.

Chelsea leaned on her pitchfork and started laughing. "Remember when Josie came to visit us?"

Allie stopped raking and snickered. They loved reminding each other about their cousin who had spent a week with them last summer.

"Remember she thought she could rake hay in shorts and a T-shirt?" continued Chelsea.

"Yeah, she thought she was going to get a tan or something," laughed Allie. "Instead, she got burned, bit and scratched up."

"I wonder why she didn't come back this summer," mused Chelsea, holding back a little smile.

"Beats me," grinned Allie.

The story helped to perk them up a bit and they built another big haystack.

Haying was hard, dirty work. Horseflies, hornets and gnats were always buzzing about. Even in the summer heat, both girls wore long pants and long-sleeved shirts to protect them from the sun, bugs and hay sticks. They had boots on their feet and hats on their heads. They worked almost every day from mid-morning until mid-afternoon.

But there was nothing better than flopping down into a bed of hay at the end of the day and breathing in its warm, sweet smell.

"It looks like Pop and Gramps are almost done baling that back lot," observed Allie.

Pop and Gramps drove tractors attached to balers. The balers scooped up the cut hay in the front end, formed it into a 60-pound square and dropped it out the back end onto the field. Then, the bales were collected and brought back to the barn and stacked in the hayloft.

Chelsea smiled. She could see Gramps' dog, Blackie, running beside his tractor.

Soon they heard the "thump, thump, thump" of the tractors rumbling toward them.

"You know what that means," said Allie.

"Lemonade break!" they shouted in unison.

Waves of heat surrounded the big green tractors and they seemed to shimmer in the distance. It looked like the exhaust stacks were belching little hot-air bubbles and the big driving wheels in the back kicked up clouds of dust.

The big machines got closer and closer and the noise got

louder and louder.

"Allie! What's Curly doing?" Chelsea grabbed Allie's shoulder and pointed her toward the enclosure. Curly was galloping crazily around the fence, throwing his head and neighing loudly.

"Chelsea!" cried Allie, "What's wrong with Toby?"

Toby had suddenly reared up, his front hooves pawing the air frantically.

Chelsea was alarmed. "Do you think the tractors spooked them?"

"No," said Allie. "They know what the tractors sound like."

Behind them, they heard shouting and honking horns. They turned to see Gramps standing up in the cab, waving his arms wildly. Blackie was barking and running in circles. Pop jumped off his tractor and was running toward them. The girls were confused. Why was everyone acting so crazy?

"Girls," shouted their father, "Open the doors to the house. Hurry!"

Chelsea threw down her pitchfork and sprinted for the house. Allie ran after her causing her hat to fly off and land upside-down on the hay bale.

"Chelsea," shouted Allie, "you get the back door and I'll get the front door."

Chelsea rounded the corner of the house and flung open the back door. As she did, something whooshed past her.

Allie threw open the front door just in time to see a little hissing ball about as big as her hand fly past her.

BANG! It exploded just outside the door.

Gramps came into the front yard with Blackie yelping at his heels.

Chelsea ran through the house and onto the porch. "Gramps, what was that?!?"

Gramps leaned heavily against the porch railing. He took off his cap and wiped his face with his red-checked bandanna.

"Girls," said Gramps, panting, "you just saw a fire ball. I swear, I haven't seen one of those darn things since I was a boy."

"What's a fire ball?" asked Chelsea.

"Well, in the old days it was called 'ball lightning.' Sometimes you'd see them during thunderstorms, sometimes not. If it hit something, it could catch fire."

"You mean it could have burned down our house?" exclaimed Allie.

Gramps chuckled. "It's best not to find out, isn't it?"

"Is that why Toby and Curly were so frightened?" Chelsea asked.

"Yep," answered Gramps. "Blackie, here, saw one coming at the tractor. They're attracted to metal. That's why your Pop and I decided to come in. We saw one rolling toward the house when we drove up."

"It looks like the only damage done is to these flowers," said Pop. He walked through the back door and into the hallway.

The force of the fire ball had knocked over a vase of flowers from an iron stand. Daisies and water covered the floor.

"Thank goodness you girls did as you were told," said Pop, "or we might be cleaning up more than just spilled flowers."

"I think we've all earned a big, tall glass of cold lemonade," said Gramps.

You won't
get burned
when you listen
to your parents.

Weather or Not

Paige felt a raindrop on her hand. When she looked up, another one splashed her forehead. By the time she made it back inside, a light rain was falling. Paige didn't mind — she liked rain and so did her flower garden.

She put a bunch of daisies cut from the garden in a vase on the kitchen table. Paige looked at her watch — it was getting late and she was supposed to meet her neighbor, Imani, to walk to school. She grabbed her book bag, plucked a daisy from the vase for her English teacher, Mrs. Gersch, and ran out the back door. She pulled up the hood on her slicker and ducked her head as she ran down the driveway.

Paige and Imani walked to school every day. They were in charge of the morning announcements at Goodale and had to get to the office early to practice reading the list of daily activities and other school news. They were a good team and enjoyed their job.

Paige stopped at the curb and saw Imani grinning at her from the other side.

"Imani, where's your umbrella? You're going to get wet," yelled Paige.

Imani just laughed and stuck out her hand.

"What rain?" she shouted back.

Paige stared at her friend who was standing directly across from her completely dry. She looked up and down the street before stepping slowly off the curb and walking to the middle of the road. Her half of the street was wet and Imani's half was dry. It was raining on one side of the street!

Paige burst out laughing.

"Isn't it crazy," laughed Imani. "I've never seen anything like it, have you?"

"No way," replied Paige.

"Come on. We can't be late," said Imani. "But I hope you don't mind if I stay on my side of the street."

Paige grinned and shook her head and they set off on their four-block walk to school. Imani squinted into the morning sun as Paige splashed through puddles. Rivulets of water ran off her slicker and into her boots, soaking her socks. When she got to the corner of Dickerson and Longview, Paige crossed over

and joined her friend.

Goodale School took up almost an entire block and was home to over 1000 students. Paige and Imani were always the first ones to arrive. They loved walking in and having the cavernous hallways all to themselves.

"Good morning, girls," said Miss Pins, their homeroom teacher. She stopped and watched as a small puddle of water formed around Paige's boots.

"Paige, I'm surprised at you," said Miss Pins. "You're a little too old to be playing in your neighbors' sprinklers."

"I didn't, Miss Pins," explained Paige. "It's raining outside," and she gestured towards the window.

Miss Pins put her hands on her hips and shook her head. "Paige, I just came in the back door and it was perfectly dry out there."

Imani rushed to defend her friend. "No, really, Miss Pins," protested Imani. "It's raining on one side of the street."

Miss Pins gave the girls a hard look. "All right! That's quite enough from both of you," she said sharply. "Follow me, please!"

The girls' mouths fell open and they glanced at each other in shock. Miss Pins didn't believe them! Paige's boots squished and squeaked as they followed her down the hall.

Miss Pins opened the door and led the girls into the empty office.

"Sit there," she said pointing to two chairs in the corner. "You can tell your story to Principal Reeves."

"But Miss Pins," said Imani, "We have to prepare for morning announcements."

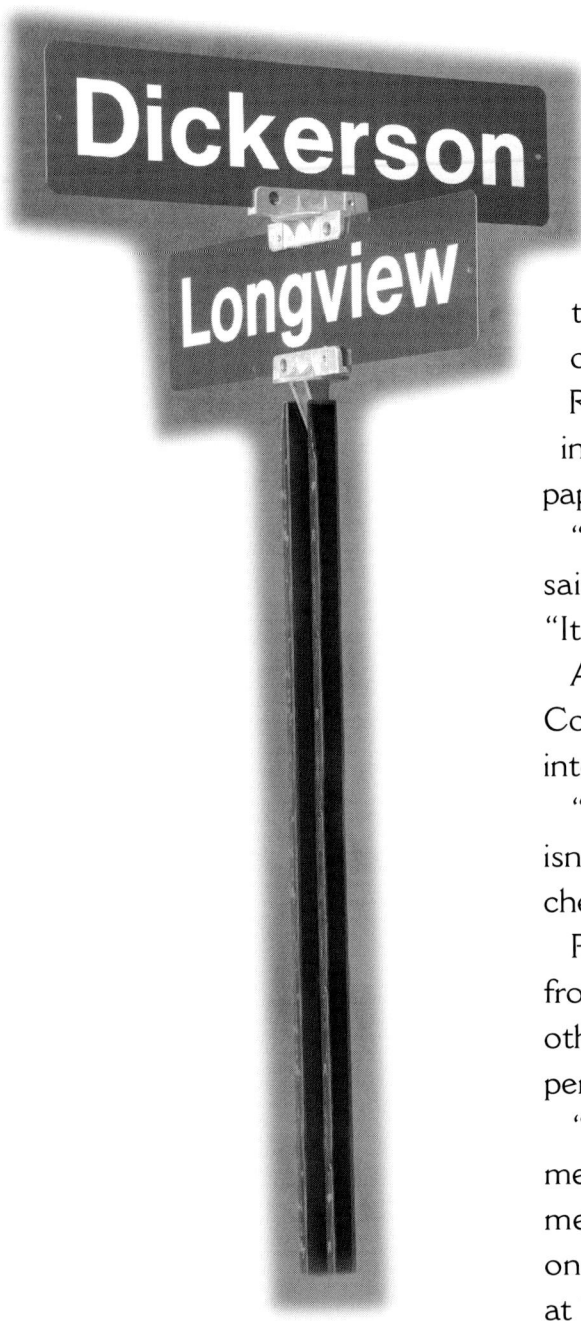

"Girls, I don't think you'll be doing that this morning."

As Miss Pins turned to leave, the office door flew open and Principal Reeves came rushing in holding a wet newspaper over her head.

"Oh my goodness," said Principal Reeves. "It's pouring out there."

A few moments later, Coach Andrey strolled into the office.

"Beautiful morning, isn't it, ladies?" he said cheerfully.

Paige and Imani looked from one adult to the other. Miss Pins looked perplexed.

"But, I ... it can't. I mean, is it?" she stammered. "What's going on, here?" she said at last.

"We tried to tell you ..." said Imani quietly.

"... That it's raining on one side of the street," continued Paige.

"But you didn't believe us," finished Imani.

The three adults and two girls walked to the front windows of the school and saw a spring rain. But when they walked to the back windows, they saw a dry, sunny day.

"I don't believe it," said Principal Reeves.

"I didn't either," said an embarrassed Miss Pins. "Girls, I owe you a big apology. I thought your story was all wet. I really should have given you the benefit of the doubt."

Principal Reeves chuckled. "In a way their story was all wet," she said. "Or at least half of it. Wasn't it, girls?"

Paige and Imani just smiled.

The office sat in the middle of the hallway and the group could see students arriving from both the front and back doors. The front half were wearing raincoats and carrying umbrellas while the back half were dressed for fair weather.

As they crossed paths, their delighted chatter reached an excited pitch.

"Well, everyone, I think it's going to be a very interesting morning," said Principal Reeves. "Girls, are you ready to give the morning announcements?"

"You mean, we can?" they asked hopefully.

"Of course," said the principal, "after all you were first on the scene, weren't you?"

Paige and Imani dashed off to the room where the microphone was set up. Imani flipped the switch to its "on" position. Then they both leaned in and began the morning address.

61

"Good morning, Goodale students ..."

Goodale
School
Morning
Announcements

Shower people
with understanding
for there are
two sides to every story.

Fishing for Success

A melia balanced herself on the rocky ledge as she dipped her bucket into the school of minnows swimming in the shallow part of the lake. When she hauled it up, the bucket was filled with dozens of the little fish.

"These will make great bait for the bigger fish," she said excitedly to her friend.

Olivia winced — first earthworms, now minnows. She wasn't too sure about this fishing stuff. She held her pole as Amelia hooked one of the silvery fish onto her line.

"Gross, Amelia," she said disgustedly.

Amelia rolled her eyes. "Olivia, this is how you catch fish — with fish food. Now throw your line into the water while I lock our bikes."

She pulled the key out of her top pocket by its braided strap and hiked up to the bikes.

Olivia cast her line just like Amelia had taught her. She liked the whirring sound the line made as it spun out quickly from the reel. And she liked the feel of the pole in her hands when the line — with the squirming bait — smacked the top of the water.

The round, red and white bobbin kept the bait floating just below the surface. Amelia returned and explained to Olivia how she would know if a fish were only nibbling at the bait.

"The bobbin will bob," she said simply. "So slowly reel in your line. The fish will think the bait is swimming away and it might bite it instead."

Olivia watched the bobbin carefully. Part of her hoped the fish weren't biting today.

"But, Olivia," said Amelia emphatically, "if the bobbin completely disappears, that means a fish has swallowed the bait and probably the hook, too."

Olivia's eyes widened. "What do I do then?" she asked worriedly.

"Just give the pole a sharp tug. That sets the hook in the fish's mouth. Then reel it in as fast as you can."

Olivia gave Amelia a horrified look. Set the hook! That sounded perfectly awful. That poor fish, she thought. Couldn't they do something else like collecting clamshells or catching salamanders?

Olivia concentrated on the bobbin as it floated gently in the water. Suddenly, it dipped below the surface then popped back up. Was a fish nibbling, she wondered? She slowly reeled in her line.

Then, the bobbin completely disappeared beneath the surface and the pole almost flew out of her hands.

"Amelia!" she cried. "Help!"

Amelia grabbed the fishing net off the ground. The line was spinning crazily off the reel and the bobbin was racing through the water away from them. Olivia leaned backwards, struggling to hold onto the pole, and cranking the handle as hard as she could.

The pole was almost bent in half from the weight of the fish and Amelia feared it would snap.

"Reel it in closer and I'll try to catch it in the net!" she shouted.

SPLASH! A huge fish burst out of the water. It flipped in the air, trying to break free of the hook.

Amelia leaned out over the rocks and caught it in the net as it came back down toward the water.

"Got it!" she yelled. "Wow, is it heavy."

Olivia guided the pole as Amelia lifted the fish away from the water and onto land.

"Amelia, I did it! I caught a fish," gloated Olivia.

Amelia smiled and she cut the line.

"I'm going to take out the hook," said Amelia. "We don't want to hurt him so don't let him flop around."

Olivia gently placed one hand on the tail and the other on its scaly body. She watched as the pink gills opened and closed.

"He's too big to take home on our bikes," said Amelia, as she returned the fishing hook to the tackle box.

"Maybe we could put him back?" wondered Olivia.

"He was a good catch, Olivia," said Amelia.

They lifted the net together and placed it in the water. The fish slowly wiggled itself free and swam away. The girls packed up their gear and loaded it in their baskets. Amelia knelt down to unlock the bikes.

"Olivia, I can't find the key. Do you have it?" asked Amelia.

"No," answered Olivia.

Amelia dug through her pockets again and searched the tackle box. They searched the ground by the bikes but no key. Then they searched the area where they had unhooked the fish. But still no key.

Something glinted in the water. Could it be, thought Olivia? She looked down and saw the key shimmering on the bottom of the lake.

"Amelia, I found it!" she called.

Amelia ran over and peered into the water where Olivia was pointing. A school of minnows glided by and seaweed waved beneath the surface.

"It must have fallen out when I caught the fish with the net," moaned Amelia. She stretched out on the ground and plunged her arm in the water.

"It's too deep, I can't reach it," she said. Clouds of sand swirled around as she drew out her arm and for a moment they lost sight of the key.

"Maybe I should wade in and get it," suggested Olivia.

"No!" said Amelia. "That's too dangerous. Come on, let's think. There's got to be a way."

The girls sat down and pondered their problem. It would take over an hour to walk home. Plus, they'd have to carry all their fishing gear, too. Just thinking about it made Olivia tired. She idly picked the bark off a dead tree branch and threw the pieces in the water.

Seeing the branch, Amelia came up with an idea.

"If we find a long enough stick," she said, "we might be able to fish the key out of the lake by its strap."

"Good idea," said Olivia.

They jumped up and searched along the shore.

"Found one!" yelled Amelia.

The girls laid down on their stomachs and Amelia angled the stick into the murky water. She hooked the key on the first try and gently pulled it out.

"Good job, Amelia," shouted Olivia.

The key dangled by the strap from the end of the stick. Olivia reached over and grabbed it.

She wiped it off on her jeans, then handed it to Amelia.

"Looks like you had a big catch today, too," smiled Olivia.

"Except we're not throwing this one back," laughed Amelia.

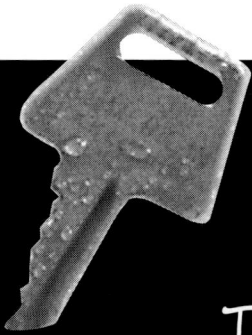

Here's the
key to success:
There's no "I"
in TEAM.

The Big Picture

"Hi, Devlin," said Ricky, greeting his friend on the sidewalk. "Did you bring your paint smock?"

They stood at the corner and waited for the safety patrol girl to let them cross.

"Yep. Brand new, too. Did you?" asked Devlin.

Ricky patted his backpack.

They crossed the street and entered Maire School. Ricky and Devlin pushed their way through the crowded hallways and entered Mr. Restum's classroom just as the morning bell rang.

"Good morning, class," said Mr. Restum.

"Good morning, Mr. Restum," they responded.

Each morning started with the Pledge of Allegiance and announcements over the school intercom.

"Today is the school art contest," said Principal Dib. "Students have the morning to finish their projects. Entries are due by lunch and winners will be announced following the afternoon recess. Good luck to all."

"All right, artists — you have until 11:30 this morning to finish your work," said Mr. Restum.

Some of Ricky and Devlin's classmates worked on papier mâché figures; others were molding clay or finishing collages. Ricky and Devlin had decided to paint a picture of an imaginary figure and decorate it with glued-on cloth and Styrofoam pieces.

They placed their canvas on the easel and squirted paint on their palettes. Ricky draped his smock over his head and tied the strings tightly behind his back. He didn't want to get any paint on his favorite pullover shirt.

"I'll start painting if you cut the cloth," suggested Devlin.

An hour later, a blue body with black antlers filled the canvas.

"The paint should be dry after recess," said Ricky and they ran outside to the playground.

The boys returned to their project after the morning break.

"Let's put our painting on the table so we can glue on the cloth and eye," Devlin suggested.

When they finished, they stood back to admire their creation.

"It's a reindeer-dog-giraffe-Cyclops," laughed Devlin.

Their figure had the body and tail of a dog, the long neck of

74

a giraffe and the head and antlers of a reindeer. They had pasted red and white strips of cloth along its body and a round piece of Styrofoam in the middle of the creature's forehead.

Mr. Restum came over. "That's a very nice mixed medium work, boys," he said.

The boys looked puzzled. "What does that mean, Mr. Restum?" they asked.

"It means you added things that aren't painted to your painted surface to make a piece of art." He pointed to the strips of cloth.

"But what's this supposed to be?" asked Mr. Restum, pointing to the white circle of Styrofoam.

"Dev, we forgot to paint the eyeball!" Ricky exclaimed.

He reached across the canvas and picked up the black paint bottle by the lid. But as he lifted it, the lid popped off and the bottle crashed down covering their project with thick, black paint.

"Oh, no," cried Ricky.

Mr. Restum, Ricky and Devlin tried to soak up the mess, but it was useless.

"You should have put the top back on when you were done using the paint," Ricky said sharply to Devlin. "You ruined our painting!"

"You should have checked it first," replied Devlin hotly. "You ruined our painting!"

The boys stared angrily at each other.

Mr. Restum looked at his watch. "Boys, pointing fingers isn't going to solve your problem. You still have twenty minutes to make something else." He walked off to help other students.

"Twenty minutes," groaned Ricky. "We'll never finish. This took us all morning."

"Way to go, Ricky," muttered Devlin. "You even splashed paint on my new smock."

Ricky was just about to yell at Devlin when he had an idea.

"Hey, Dev, take off your smock."

Ricky spread Devlin's smock flat on the table.

"What are you doing?" Devlin asked.

"Remember what Mr. Restum said about that mixed medium thing?" asked Ricky.

"Yeah. He said it was putting unpainted stuff on top of painted stuff," replied Devlin.

"Right," said Ricky. "What if we do the opposite?" He pointed to the black paint splattered on the smock. "Instead of cloth on top of paint, we put paint on top of cloth."

Devlin gave Ricky a broad smile. "That's a great idea," he said. "What can I do?"

"I'll paint dots all around the edges," offered Ricky, "if you drip paint all over the front."

The boys worked quickly and intently.

Mr. Restum came over to their table.

"Well, it looks like you two worked things out," he said.

"Class," he announced, "time's up. Please clean up your work areas and take your projects to the library for judging."

Devlin helped Ricky tack their painted smock to a big piece of cardboard.

"It looks great, Ricky," said Devlin. "Sorry, about not putting the top back on the paint."

"I shouldn't have picked it up that way," answered Ricky.

They carried their project to the library and went to lunch.

It was hard to concentrate on their schoolwork that afternoon; everyone was thinking about the contest. Finally, it was time to announce the winners. Dr. Dib addressed the school over the intercom.

"Students, all the entries were excellent. The winning projects will be on display in the library all week. Please join me in congratulating the following people."

Dr. Dib read the names of all the winners. Ricky and Devlin looked at each other sadly. They didn't win anything!

"And, finally, in the area of mixed medium work," continued Dr. Dib, "the first-place ribbon is awarded to Ricky and Devlin in Mr. Restum's class."

Mr. Restum and the class cheered and Ricky high-fived Devlin across the table.

After school, the boys dashed up the two flights of stairs to the library. A bright blue ribbon hung on Devlin's smock.

"Hey, I think I see some black paint on our ribbon," joked Ricky. "Did you put it there, Dev?"

"Nope. I'm pretty sure it was your fault, Ricky."

And they both laughed.

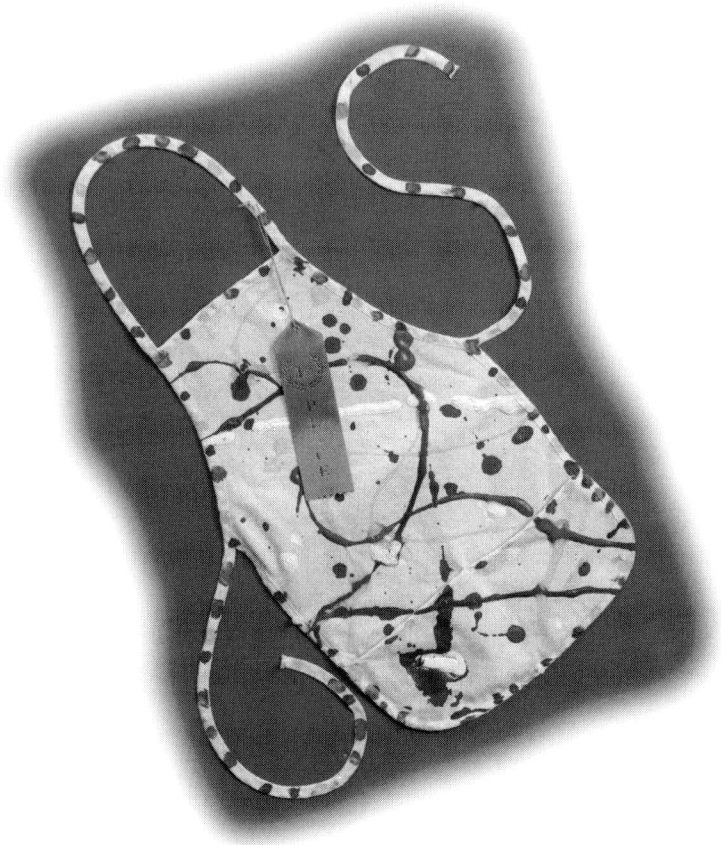

You're always
a winner when you
take responsibility
for your actions.

1st PLACE

A Chilling Tale

Katie jumped out of bed and ran to the window. Snow drifted up the side of the barn and covered the stone bunny in the garden.

"Katie, breakfast," called her Mom. The smell of pancakes wafted up the stairs. She dressed quickly, pulling on her favorite sweater.

"Can I go sledding with Leah?" she asked as she slid into her chair at the table next to her Dad, who had just finished his morning coffee.

"Sure, honey," said Mrs. Monette. "Just be home in time for lunch."

Katie ate a stack of pancakes covered with warm maple syrup. She cleared her plate before pulling on her snow pants, boots, hat and gloves.

"See you later," she called over her shoulder as she shut the kitchen door behind her. She grabbed her Flyer sled from the barn and headed for the sledding hill.

Neighbors Kevin, Collin, Henry and John were waiting their turns at the top of the hill and Katie took her place at the back of the line. Her best friend Leah pushed off on her toboggan with cousins Ellie and Maizie riding along behind her. They screamed and laughed all the way down the long, steep slope.

"It's really fast," Kevin warned Katie as he plopped down on his snow saucer. Halfway down, his saucer spun around and Kevin finished sliding down the hill backwards — whooping wildly all the way. His sled coasted to a stop in front of Mr. Neff's house, which sat right at the bottom of the hill. The front door opened.

"Young man, you are making way too much noise," scolded Mr. Neff. He glared at the other kids at the top of the hill. "Keep your voices down!" He bellowed, before stomping inside.

"Gosh, we're just trying to have fun," griped Katie to Leah.

"Yeah, I know," panted Leah, who was out of breath from pulling her toboggan back up the hill. "He's yelled at us a couple of times already."

They sledded until the sun started turning the snow to slush.

"Last runs," hollered Kevin.

Leah gave Katie a big push. "Whoopee!" yelled Katie as her

sled careened down the hill. Her eyes were watering and her cheeks were stinging from the cold air. She dragged her boots behind the sled to make it stop.

"That was great! Bet you can't make it this far, Leah," shouted Katie. She saw Mr. Neff scowling at her from his front window.

Leah jumped on her toboggan and barreled down the hill. When she realized she was going too fast to stop, she rolled off. The toboggan rushed on without her and crashed into Mr. Neff's front door.

He stormed out, dragged the toboggan inside his house and slammed the door shut.

The other kids came running down the hill.

"What happened?" asked Maizie.

"Mr. Neff took Leah's sled," stammered Katie.

"Leah, knock on the door and ask him to give it back," suggested Ellie.

"Yeah, just say you're sorry," said Henry.

"We'll go with you," said John.

"You can borrow my sled, Leah," offered Collin.

"I think I better go home and tell my Dad," said a shaken Leah, adjusting her earmuffs that had come off during her tumble from the toboggan.

"I'll walk home with you," Kevin said.

Everyone went home except Katie. She couldn't believe what had just happened and felt bad for her friend, Leah. That Mr. Neff is nothing but a big bully, thought Katie angrily. He should pick on somebody his own size. Size! That gave Katie an idea and she raced back up the hill. She knelt down and

made a
snow-
ball and
pushed it
through
the snow
until it was
as big as a
basketball.
She rolled the
snowball to the
edge of the hill and
aimed it right for Mr.
Neff's house. Then she
gave the snowball a
shove and it rolled
and it rolled and it
rolled down the
hill getting bigger
and bigger and
bigger until it
smacked into
his front door.

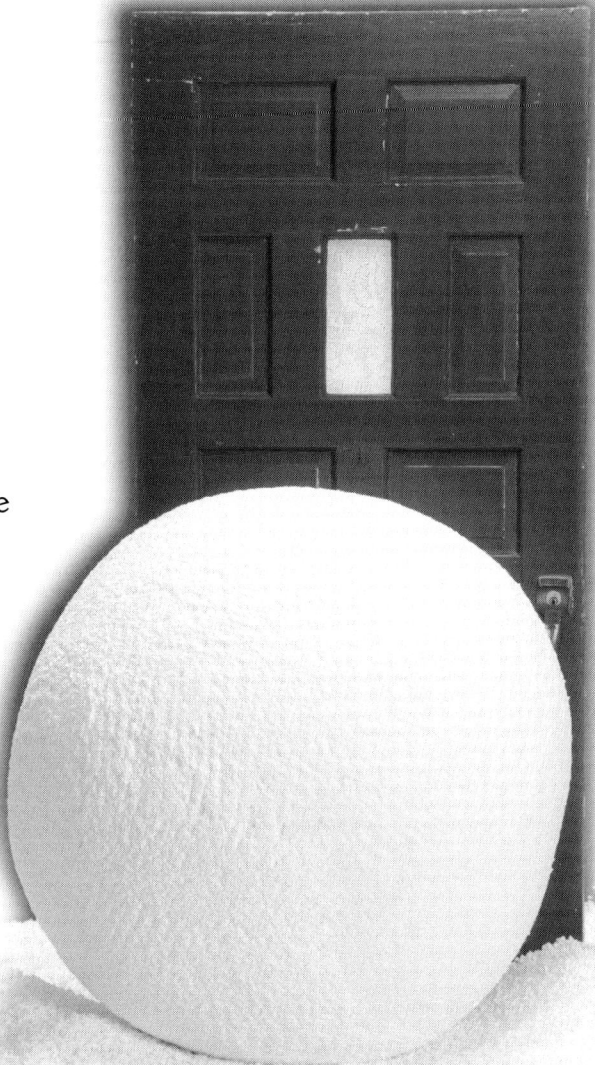

Katie was shocked. She hadn't really expected the snowball to hit its target. She grabbed the Flyer's rope and took off running for home.

"Why, you're just in time for lunch," said Mrs. Monette as Katie rushed into the kitchen. "I made grilled cheese — your favorite."

Katie sat at the table but only poked at her sandwich.

"What's the matter, honey?" asked Mrs. Monette. She brushed aside Katie's soft, red hair and felt her forehead. It was hot and moist. "Don't you feel well?" she asked.

Katie didn't look up and she felt a lump forming in her throat. "Mom, I did something really mean." She told her Mom about sledding, the shouting and the snowball.

"I think you know what you need to do," said her Mom firmly.

Katie pushed her chair back from the table and put on her boots. She picked up a shovel from the barn and headed back to Mr. Neff's house. Along the way, she ran into her friend Leah.

"Hi, Leah. What's up?" asked Katie.

"I'm going to Mr. Neff's house to apologize about hitting his door with my toboggan," Leah said. "What are you doing?"

"I'm going to apologize, too," said Katie.

"What for?" asked Leah.

Katie told Leah about the snowball. "Now I have to dig it all out," she sighed.

"Wait here," yelled Leah and she ran back toward her house. She reappeared a few minutes later with her shovel.

The two friends shoveled the wet, heavy snow all afternoon. Finally, they cleared the last pile from the doorway and knocked. Mr. Neff opened the door. They could see Leah's toboggan propped up against his living room wall.

"Mr. Neff, I'm sorry I hit your house with my toboggan," said Leah.

"And I'm sorry I got mad and rolled that snowball against your door," said Katie.

"Your apologies are accepted," Mr. Neff said curtly. He handed Leah her toboggan and shut the door.

The girls looked at each other puzzled, then shrugged.

"I bet he's sorry that he took your toboggan, Leah. He just forgot to say so," smiled Katie.

"I bet you're right," laughed Leah. The two friends threw the shovels over their shoulders and headed for home.

Don't get snowed
into thinking
that two wrongs
make a right.

87

In Too Deep

"Dad! Dad! Stop the car!"

Mr. Gee slammed on the brakes and the car lurched to a stop.

"What the ... what's the matter, Meredith?"

Mr. Gee turned to look at his daughter but she was already running up the driveway toward the house.

He smiled as he watched her go — losing one rhinestone flip-flop and then the other. Meredith burst into the kitchen as her Mom came up from the basement.

"Mom, I almost forgot these!" Meredith grabbed her swim goggles off the counter and put them on her head. They had blue eyepieces with a fluorescent green strap and Meredith never went to the pool without them.

"I think you forgot something else."

"Oh, yeah," laughed Meredith. She gave her Mom a big hug.

"Be careful and have fun," said Mrs. Gee, kissing the top of her daughter's head.

Meredith ran back to the car scooping up her flip-flops along the way. Mr. Gee backed out of the driveway and they drove off to the City Pool.

It was a beautiful summer morning and the pool was packed. Meredith waved to her friends who were already in the water. "Come on, Meredith," they called. "We're diving for rings."

"Go ahead," said Mr. Gee, as he shielded his eyes from the sun. "But remember, you aren't allowed past the blue lane marker. That's the deep end and you're not a good enough swimmer yet. Stay in the shallow end."

"I know, Dad. I know," said an exasperated Meredith.

"All right, get going. I'll fix lunch."

Meredith jumped in the pool and joined her friends Emily, Julie and Lisa. They knew she couldn't swim very well, so they let her wear goggles and gave her the first turn at hiding the rings.

"Close your eyes, guys." Meredith hid the pink ring behind the pool ladder, the green ring in the pool gutter and the blue ring in a corner.

"One, two, three, GO!" yelled Meredith.

Her friends swam around searching for the rings. Emily found the pink ring and Julie found the green ring, but no one could find the blue ring.

"Give up?" asked Meredith.

Just then, Emily spied it. "Got it," she shouted. "I win. It's my turn."

They played all morning but Meredith still hadn't had another turn hiding the rings when her Dad called her for lunch.

"Let's play one more game," suggested Lisa.

Meredith closed her eyes. I hope I find a ring this time, she thought.

"One, two, three, GO!" yelled Lisa.

Meredith looked around as Emily and Julie dove underwater.

"Got one," called Julie as she surfaced with the pink ring.

"Me, too," sputtered Emily as she held up the green ring.

Meredith frowned. If I were a better swimmer I wouldn't always come in last! Then, she saw it. Lisa had hidden the blue ring right on top of the blue lane marker that separated the shallow end from the deep end. How sneaky, Meredith thought to herself.

Meredith waded over to the lane marker. But when she reached for the ring, it slid off and slowly floated into the deep end.

"Oh, no," said Meredith.

She put her face in the water. Her goggles made everything seem so clear and close. I can get it, she thought, it's not that far away.

Meredith took a deep breath and dove under the lane marker. She grabbed the drifting blue ring firmly with her right hand. I got you! But when she tried to stand up, nothing was there. Uh oh, thought Meredith.

She sank straight to the bottom. With her goggles on, Meredith could see everything underwater, including her friends who were still looking for the blue ring in the shallow end.

I'll just push myself to the top and swim to the side, reasoned Meredith. She shoved off the bottom as hard as she could.

She broke through the surface and tried to take a breath. But instead, she swallowed a little bit of water and started choking. She panicked and started sinking again. Glub, glub, glub, went Meredith as little bubbles escaped from her nose. She pushed off the bottom again and shot back to the surface. Now she was too tired and out of breath to stay afloat and sank for a third time.

Her bottom lip quivered and her goggles filled with tears. She wished she hadn't reached for that dumb ring. She wished she had listened to her Dad and not gone in the deep end. She was very scared. What am I going to do, she thought frantically.

Meredith looked up and saw a pool floatie land directly above her. She had an idea and blasted up — right into the middle of the floatie. She grabbed its sides gasping for air when the blue ring fell out of her hand and floated to the bottom of the pool.

"NO!" shouted Meredith. But it was gone. She kicked her way to the side of the pool and climbed out. Mrs. Shay, her next-door neighbor, came running over to her.

"The wind just blew that into the pool, Meredith. Thanks for getting it for Stephanie." Mrs. Shay smiled and took the floatie from an exhausted Meredith and handed it to her daughter.

Meredith saw her Dad and her friends on the pool deck and dragged herself over to them.

"There you are. We've been looking for you," exclaimed Mr. Gee.

Meredith told them about going into the deep end and

being rescued by the floatie. "It all happened so fast, Dad. I was really scared."

Mr. Gee listened quietly. "Meredith," he said, "I told you not to go in the deep end, didn't I? That was dangerous. Do you know why we have rules like that for you?"

Meredith shook her head.

"Because we love you and we want you to be safe."

Meredith looked down at the pool deck. "Sorry, Dad," she whispered.

Mr. Gee nodded as he draped her favorite green-and-white-striped towel around her shoulders.

"Well, I'm glad you're all right. I think you learned a pretty important lesson today."

Meredith put her hands on her hips and said firmly, "Dad, I think I'd like to take swim lessons."

"I think that's a great idea," said Mr. Gee. "We'll sign you up after lunch, OK?"

"OK!" said Meredith.

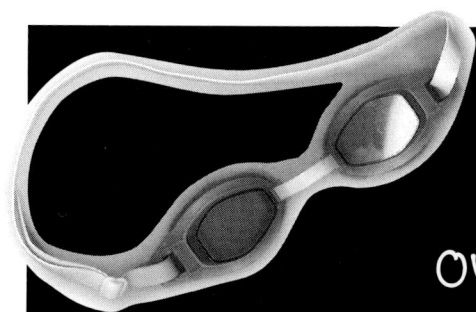

Don't get in
over your head:
Follow directions.

About the Authors

Snip Francis and Melanie Gilbert are the co-authors of
Hey Look! The Happy Book, a children's picture book
of rhyming text, also published by Little Salamander Press.
They are Michigan natives who draw inspiration for their
stories from the people and events that fill their world.

The End